Izzi Kidding

Jokes, Wisecracks, & Shenanigans
for People 12 to 103

Compiled & Curated
by

**Izzi Tooinsky,
king of Hotdogastan**

Izzi Kidding: Jokes, Wisecracks, and Shenanigans for People 12 to 103
First edition published November 15, 2025.

Published by Cabanga, an imprint of Royall, LLC.
128 Race St., Grass Valley, CA 95945
+1 (808) 301-0535

In association with the Hotdogastan Jugglers Guild.

ISBN 979-8-9914547-9-7 Paperback

For copyright permissions contact Cabanga
or visit www.izzitooinsky.com for more information.

Cover art by R.S. Royall and Izzi Tooinsky.

Thank you for purchasing this book. The Royall agency is a small business. You can help us continue to deliver quality content by posting a review online, referring us to your local library or bookstore, and, most importantly, sharing this book with a friend. Be sure to check out other books by Cabanga Press such as A Teenager's Compass to Life by Izzi Tooinsky, and Do You Know the Slothalo? by R.S. Royall.

Babies and Kids

"Having a child is like getting a tattoo on your face. You'd better be committed." – Elizabeth Gilbert

"When my kids become wild and unruly, I use a nice, safe play pen. When they're finished, I climb out."
– Erma Bombeck

I sat next to a baby on a 10-hour flight. I didn't think it was possible for someone to cry for 10 hours straight. Even the baby was impressed I pulled it off.

If little Danny refuses to take a nap, does that mean he is resisting a rest?

What do you call a group of baby soldiers? An infantry.

Mrs. Goat: "Honey, we're going to have a baby!"
Mr. Goat: "You're kidding!"

What's the difference between broccoli and boogers?
Kids won't eat broccoli.

My house is supposed to be kid safe.
Somehow they still get in.

Do you know why babies born on holidays are more than likely to be girls? There's no mail delivery on holidays.

Sometimes I wake up grumpy. Other times I just let him sleep.

People who tell you they sleep like a baby probably don't have one.

We were so poor when I was a kid, my mom would sit us down at the table, bring out a big cookbook, and just read the recipes to us. We had a little brother who was so hard of hearing that he nearly starved to death!

When I was a kid, we were so poor even our rainbows were in black and white.

When I was a kid, we were so poor that my dad would take us to KFC so that we could lick other people's fingers.

A baby's laugh is one of the most beautiful things you will ever hear… unless it is 3 a.m., you're home alone... and you don't have a baby.

"I've been pregnant for so long it feels like a maternity!"

Ending childhood obesity is as easy as taking candy from a baby.

Buck: What does your father do for a living?
Willy: He is a magician. He cuts people in two.
Buck: Do you have any brothers or sisters?
Willy: Well, I have a half-brother and a half-sister.

Memo: "The 8th graders will be presenting Shakespeare's Hamlet in the church on Friday at 7 pm. The congregation is invited to attend the tragedy."

I asked my mom if I was adopted. She said, "Not yet, but the ad has only been in the paper a week." - Dana Snow

Children may be deductible, but they're still taxing.

Hell hath no fury like a toddler whose sandwich has been cut into squares when they wanted triangles.

In what state was Abraham Lincoln born? Naked and screaming, just like the rest of us.

A mom and her boy were at church. The little guy said, "Mom, I have to pee." The mother replied quietly, "Don't say the word pee in church. It's not nice. Instead, say you have to *whisper*." The next Sunday the boy was at church with his dad. He tapped him on the shoulder and said, "Dad, I have to *whisper*." Surprised, the father quietly said, "Ok, just *whisper* in my ear."

A nine-year-old girl disappeared after using moisturizer that makes you look ten years younger.

5

Fred: "Would you like to have children *one* day."
Gracie: "Yes. Possibly even longer than that."

No one makes more observations than a child sharing a stall with his mother or father inside a public restroom.

I asked my wife if she wanted me to pick up Fish and Chips on the way home. She just groaned and hung up. I think she's still mad at me for naming the twins.

Cars, Moving Vehicles, & Traveling

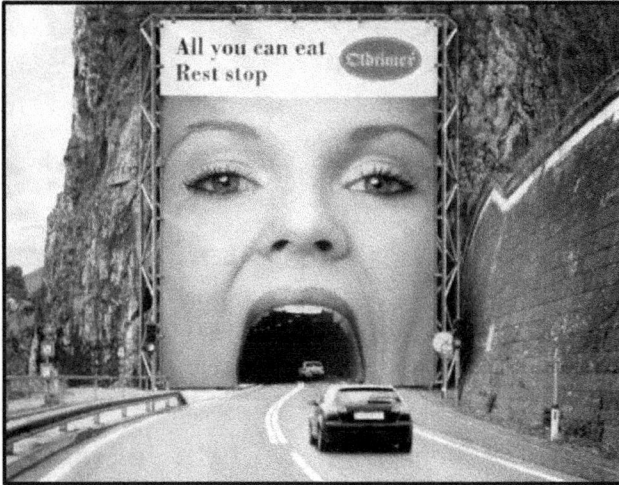

Last night I dreamt I was a muffler. I woke up exhausted.

"Honey, I have good news and bad news about the car."
"Give me the good news first."
"The airbags work."

What did the cowgirl say when she walked into the German car dealership? "Audi!"

I was driving my motorcycle past a farm and saw a sign that said, "Duck, eggs." I thought, *that's an unnecessary comma.* And then it hit me.

I want to die peacefully in my sleep, like my grandfather. Not screaming and yelling like the other passengers in his car.

What did the tornado say to the sports car?
How about we go for a little spin.

News Flash: Willie Nelson got hit by a car last night. He was playing on the road again.

Disturbulence: When you need some sleep, but the airline passenger next to you won't shut up.

Husband: "Honey, look at that. The neighbor is washing his car with his son again!"
Wife: "Poor kid! I'm going over there right this minute to tell the neighbor to use a sponge instead."

My wife is so negative. One day, I remembered the car seat, the stroller, AND the diaper bag, but all she can talk about is how I forgot the baby.

What do you call a paper airplane that can't fly? Stationary.

Why don't aliens visit our planet? Because Earth has terrible ratings; only one star.

I'm not too good at geography, but I can name at least one city in France. That's Nice.

There's a new film coming out about the incorrect use of tow bars on cars. The trailer just dropped.

How do crazy hikers get out of the forest? They take the *psycho* path.

Law and Disorder

The guy who stole my diary just died.
My thoughts are with his family.

They say that mafia members are bad people, but as a kid I lived next door to one and he was actually very nice. Every morning, he paid me $20 just to start his car.

Breaking News: The tongue twister champion of the world just got arrested. He was given a tough sentence.

A cement mixer and a prison bus collided. Police advise citizens to look out for a group of hardened criminals.

I saw a dwarf climbing down a prison wall and thought, *that's a little con descending.*

I told my mom that thieves had stolen 20 crates of Red Bull from the supermarket. She said, "I don't know how these people sleep at night."

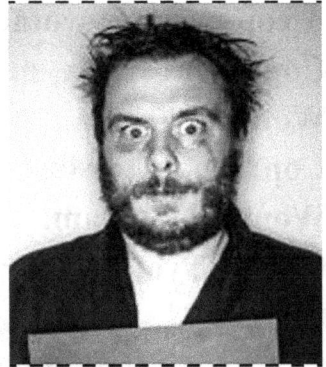

A man ran into a bank, took out his gun, and screamed, "Everyone get on the floor or you're geography!" A middle-school teacher dropped to the floor and said, "Don't you mean history?" The robber snapped back, "Don't change the subject!"

There was a break-in at the police station today and the toilet was stolen. The police have nothing to go on.

Headline: Energizer Bunny arrested, charged with battery.

News Flash: A vandal smashed a large hole in the wall around The Sunny Side Nudist Colony. Police are still looking into it.

Why is it tricky to plan a bank robbery with pigs? They always squeal.

What kind of phones do convicts use? Cell phones!

A cop pulled a woman over.
Cop: Your name, ma'am?
Woman: Freida.
Cop: And your last name?
Woman: Gomam.
Cop: So, you're... Freida Gomam?
"Thanks!" she said, and sped off.

Someone stole my mood ring yesterday. I still don't know how I feel about it.

Breaking: Someone swiped the wheels off all the local police squad cars. Police are searching tirelessly for the perpetrator.

A jar of white makeup was stolen from the local department store. The police are interrogating a mime, but he's not talking.

Officer: "I noticed your eyes are bloodshot. Have you been drinking?"
Driver: "I noticed your eyes are glazed over. Have you been eating donuts?"

Officer: "Why'd you park here?
Joe: "The sign says, 'Fine for parking.'"

Officer: "Do you know why I pulled you over?"
Lorraine: "You were bored and wanted some company?"

What happens when a police officer goes to bed? He becomes an undercover cop.

An officer pulled a man over and noticed he was not wearing his required prescription glasses.
Officer: "I have to give you a ticket for driving without your glasses."
Driver: "Officer, I have contacts."
Officer: "I don't care who you know, you're getting a ticket!"

Did you hear about the thief that stole a calendar? He got 12 months.

"Has anyone here been caught thieving in Saudi Arabia? Let's see a show of hands." - Jimmy Carr

Countries, States, Cities, and Cultures

How Long is a Chinese Name.

What happens when the smog lifts over Southern California? U.C.L.A.

A Mexican magician claimed he could disappear on the count of three. He said, "Uno, dos..." and then disappeared without a tres.

I asked my North Korean friend how life was going there. He looked over both shoulders and whispered, "I can't complain."

How was Rome split in two? With a pair of Caesars.

What do frogs eat in Paris? French flies.

I've heard that Argentina is starting to get a little colder.
In fact, it's bordering on Chile.

Ever since my girlfriend moved to Siberia, she's been so
cold and distant.

My friend Bjorn lived in a place that had six months of
sunlight followed by six months of complete darkness.
There is Norway I could live there.

What is the Scandinavian word for constipation?
Farfrompoopin.

I would like to go to Holland someday.
Wooden Shoe?

Which country's capital is growing the fastest?
Ireland. Every day it's Dublin.

In which country is Prague located? Hold on, let me Czech.

How did the Irish Jig get started?
Too much punch and not enough restrooms.

The weather turned cold in Palm Springs,
so the Sunny Side Nudist Colony put up a sign:
"We're open but we are clothed."

In Hawaii it's illegal to laugh loudly.
You have to keep it at A-lo-ha.

What's the best thing about Switzerland?
Well, to start with, their flag is a big plus.

How many trees are in the Amazon rainforest?
A Brazilian.

Why do North Koreans draw the best straight lines?
They have a supreme ruler.

Some people think we should put a cap on immigrants
coming into the country, but I think people ought to be
allowed to wear any sort of hat they like!

What do you call the wife of a hippie? Mississippi.

A crowd from Japan, Korea, China, Vietnam, Mongolia, Burma, Cambodia, Philippines, Singapore, and Malaysia walked into a bar in New York City. The snooty bartender stopped them at the door and sneered, "Sorry, but I can't let you in without a Thai."

Why do all Swedish military ships have bar codes on them? So when they come to port, they can just Scan da navy in.

Creatures Large and Small

I took the shell off my racing snail, thinking it would make him faster, but if anything, it just made him more sluggish.

Two fish in a tank: The clownfish turns to the goldfish and says, "You know how to drive this thing?"

Bigfoot is often called Sasquatch,
Yeti never complains.

A new study recently found that humans eat more bananas than monkeys.
I agree. I can't remember the last time I ate a monkey.

Why wouldn't the lobster share food with her sister?
Because she was a little shellfish.

Why did the elephants get kicked out of the public pool?
They kept dropping their trunks!

Why do French people eat snails? They don't like fast food.

When will the baby snake arrive?
I don't know, but he shouldn't be long.

Two fish in a tank: One turns to the other and says,
"I'll drive, you shoot."

Which Shakespearean play does a pig like the most?
Hamlet.

Why should you never fight a dinosaur?
You'll get jurasskicked.

What has four legs and says, "AAAAAAAAA?"
A sheep with no lips.

A naked woman was being chased by a bear in Yellowstone National Park. She ran into the ranger station where they promptly arrested her. Apparently it's illegal to run through the park with a bear behind.

What did the snail say while riding on the turtle's back? "Weeeeee!"

A horse walked into a bar. "Hey," the bartender yelled. The horse looked up in surprise & said, "How did you know what I wanted to order?"

Billy: Wow, that's a cool-looking cow!
Sally: It's a Jersey.
Billy: Is it? Oh, I thought that was its skin.

Where do hip hamsters go on vacation? Hamsterdam.

Why is animal testing bad?
The animals get nervous and give all the wrong answers.

How did the mouse feel after the cat chased it through a screen door? Strained.

How do you keep a bull from charging?
Take away its credit card!

A farmer tried to sell us his bull but I didn't buy it.
He was charging too much.

What is a cat's favorite breakfast? Mice Krispies.

Comfort INN

NOW PET FRIENDLY! EXCEPT FOR BEARS. WE'RE NOT MAKING THAT MISTAKE AGAIN.

What kind of bee gives milk? A boo bee.

Why don't sharks eat lawyers? Professional courtesy.

"My uncle had a rabbit's foot for 30 years. The other foot was quite normal." - Tom Griffin

What did the fish say when he swam into a wall? "Dam."

What did the buffalo say when his son left for school? "Bye Son."

As we were getting in bed, my wife asked if I had taken the garbage out. I said I'd do it in the morning. She said, "What about the cat?" I answered, "I don't think he can manage it."

A man heard a knock at his door, opened it, and saw a small snail on the porch. He picked up the snail and threw it as far as he could. Three years later there was another knock at the door. The man opened it and saw the same snail. The snail looked up and yelled, "What the heck was that all about?"

Why did the cowboy put hay under his pillows? To feed the night-mares.

I called Marineland and got a recorded message that said, "Calls may be recorded for training porpoises."

Creatures That Flutter & Fly

I went to the beekeeper to get 12 bees. He counted them up and gave me 13. I said, "Sir, you gave me an extra one." He said, "That's a free Bee."

How do you get down from an elephant? You don't. You get down from a goose.

Why can't you hear a pterodactyl go to the bathroom? The "P" is silent!

What is a wolf that uses bad language? A swear wolf.

My wife told me to stop acting like a flamingo. So, I had to put my foot down.

Why did the chicken go to the séance?
To get to the other side.

What do you call birds that stick together? Vel-crows.

"People are saying you sound like an owl."

"Who?"

What kind of math do Owls like? Owlgebra.

I ordered a chicken and an egg from the internet. I'll let you know which comes first.

What's the difference between a chicken and a plum? They're both purple... except for the chicken.

What did they say about the dog that only ate garlic? His bark was worse than his bite.

Why did the cows go to Broadway? They wanted to see the moosicals.

What did the waiter say when he brought the dog his dinner? Bone Appetit!

A pony walked into a bar and said, "Hi Bartender, can I have a beer?" The bartender says, "I can't hear you. Speak up!" "I'm sorry," said the pony. "I'm a little hoarse."

Scientists have been studying the effect of cannabis on seabirds. They've left no Tern unstoned.

Which bird is always out of breath? A puffin!

How did the Emu get so strong? Lots of Egg-cercise.

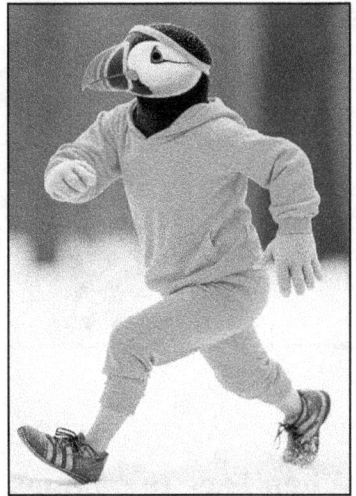

Why do seagulls fly over the sea? Because if they flew over the bay, they'd be baygulls.

Why did the vulture cross the road? The chicken didn't make it.

DARK HUMOR

Did you hear about the butcher who backed into his meat grinder? He got a little behind in his work.

Deep sleep prevents aging, especially if you are driving.

I started crying when dad was cutting up Onions.
Onions was such a good dog.

How do you make a dog drink? Put 'em in a blender.

When I see the names of lovers engraved in a tree, I don't think it's romantic. I find it strange how many people bring knives on dates.

This is my step ladder. I never met my real ladder.

What's yellow and can't swim? A dead goldfish.

I have a fish that can breakdance! But only for 20 seconds, and only once.

Henry died because we didn't know his blood type. As he was dying he kept grabbing us and wheezing, "Be positive. Be positive." Even in the end he was looking out for others. We're sure going to miss him.

Will glass coffins be a success? Remains to be seen.

A guy tried to sell me a coffin. I told him that's the *last* thing I need!

What did Kermit the Frog say at his puppeteer's funeral? Nothing.

What's the worst time to have a heart attack? During a game of charades.

Suzie: "Grandpa, can you make a sound like a frog?"
Grandpa: "Well, I can try, but why?"
Suzie: "Because grandma says we get to go to Disneyland when you croak."

I saw a sweet, little homeless woman sitting on the curb and asked if I could take her home. She smiled at me and said, "Sure!" My how the look on her face changed when I walked off with her cardboard box!

What did the cow say to the leather jacket? "Hi Mom."

What's the difference between a Ferrari and a dead body? I don't have a Ferrari in my garage.

My son was chewing on electrical cords, so I grounded him.

Never break someone's heart, they only have one.
But they do have 206 bones...

Little Mary: Excuse me, do you sell rabbits here?
Pet Shop Owner: Yes. Would you like a fuzzy white one or a fuzzy black one?
Little Mary: I don't think my python really cares.

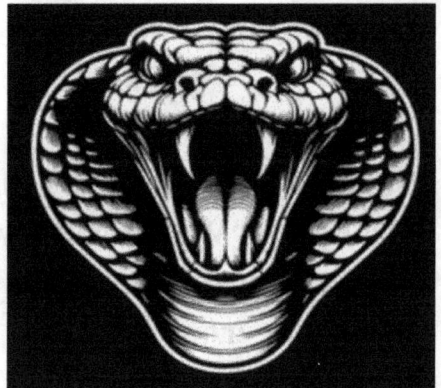

Dogs

Joe: "Hello, SPCA? I just found a suitcase filled with a dog and four puppies.
SPCA: "OMG, are they moving?"
Joe: "Oh! Of course! That would explain the suitcase."

Why did the boy name his dog Ten Miles? So he could tell his gym teacher he walked Ten Miles every day.

What do you call a wild dog that meditates? An *Aware* wolf.

What did the man name his two watch dogs? Rolex and Timex.

What is the difference between a well-dressed man and a dog? The well-dressed man wears a suit, a dog just pants.

Why did the cowboy adopt a wiener dog? He wanted to get a long little doggie.

I asked my dog how his day was. He said, "Ruff."

A man walked into a zoo where the only animal in the zoo was a dog. It was a Shitzu.

A friend wanted to start collecting dogs, so I gave him a couple of pointers.

I used to be in a band called Lost Dog. You've probably seen our posters.

My dog ate a whole bag of scrabble tiles, so I took him to the vet. No word yet.

Families

My brother convinced me to donate my organs after I die. He's a man after my own heart.

An expectant, young father nervously called the hospital and was connected to a doctor. "Doctor, Doctor, my wife has gone into labor, and her contractions are only two minutes apart!" The doctor asked, "Is this her first child?" The man answered, "No, this is her husband."

I've got two wonderful children. Two out of five ain't bad.

My ex still misses me, but her aim is getting better.

Silence is golden... unless you have little kids, then it's suspicious.

Today I visited my childhood home. I asked if I could come inside because I was feeling nostalgic, but the residents refused and slammed the door in my face. My parents have never been very nice.

How can you increase the heart rate of your 75-year-old husband?
Tell him you're pregnant.

My wife went to a self-help group for compulsive talkers. It's called On & On Anon.

I'm nice to both of my wives. Isn't that bigamy?

Uncle Sonny doesn't have a beer belly, he has a liquid grain-storage facility.

Son: Dad can you explain to me what a solar eclipse is?
Dad: No Son.

Yesterday my son said to me, "Can I have a bookmark?"
I can't believe he still doesn't know my name is Bill.

My son recently took up meditation. At least it's better than just sitting around doing nothing.

A grandma was excited about her new smart phone, so she texted her granddaughter: *"Hi Sweetie, What does ILY and TTYL mean?"* The granddaughter texted back, "Too busy to talk now but: *I love you and talk to you later."* The grandma responded, "Fine. I'll ask your brother. Love you, too." The grandmother texted her grandson: "What does IDK stand for?" The boy answered, *"I don't know."* The Grandmother sulked, "OMG, nobody does!"

"Want to know what it's like having a fourth kid? Imagine you're drowning, then someone hands you a baby." - Jim Gaffigan.

The first 40 years of parenthood are always the hardest.

Whenever I have a headache, I take two aspirins and follow the directions on the bottle: keep children away.

Edith: "My son came to visit for summer vacation."
Ethel: "How nice! Did you meet him at the airport?"
Edith: "Oh, no. I've known him since he was born!"

I really have to hand it to my grandma. Otherwise she can't reach anything.

As I handed my Dad his 50th birthday card, he looked at me with tears in his eyes and said, "You know, one would have been enough."

Where there's a will, there's a relative.

Angry Mother: "Don't talk back to me!"
Son: "But Ma, that's how a conversation works."

Wendy: "Should I have another baby after 35?"
Sandy: "No! 35 kids is enough, don't you think?"

What did the mama cow say to the baby cow?
"It's pasture bedtime."

A teenager brought her new boyfriend home to meet her parents. They were disturbed by his haircut, tattoos, and piercings. The mother said to her daughter, "Dear, he doesn't seem to be a very nice boy." "Oh, please, mom!" said the daughter. "If he wasn't nice, why would he be doing 500 hours of community service?"

I enjoy eating my family and not using commas.

My family gatherings are like fudge: mostly sweet with a few nuts here and there.

Food & Drink

What's a robot's favorite snack? Computer chips.

Yesterday I ate a kid's meal at McDonald's. Her mother was not happy.

Did you hear about the cheese factory that exploded in France? There was nothing left but de Brie.

Why did the ghost haunt the liquor shop on Halloween? For the boos.

I was on a diabetes awareness website, and it asked me if I accept cookies. Is this a trick question?

What is the favorite fruit of twins? Pears.

What does a tea pot say when
it's feeling sorry for itself?
Pour me!

It's a five-minute walk from
my house to the bar but it's a 35-minute walk
from the bar to my house. The difference is
staggering.

Why don't cannibals eat comedians?
Because they taste funny.

Why did the little cookie cry?
His dad was a wafer so long.

How did the Burger King
propose to his girlfriend? He gave her an onion ring.

RIP boiling water. You shall be mist.

I'd like to tell you a joke about this girl I know who only
eats plants. You've probably never heard of herbivore.

Who is green and sings Rock and Roll? Elvis Parsley.

Two peanuts were walking down the street in a bad part of town. One was ok, but the other one was assaulted.

What happens when you boil a funny bone? It becomes a laughing stock.

Save the Earth. It's the only planet with chocolate.

Billy asked, "Hey Dad. What's a forklift?" Dad answered,

Food, usually!

Did you hear about the new restaurant on the moon? Great food but no atmosphere.

Why did the cannibal eat the tightrope walker? He wanted a balanced meal.

A lion might never drive drunk, but a Tiger Wood.

A balanced diet is a cupcake in each hand.

Winnie the waitress asked, "Wanna box for your leftovers?" Harry the hipster answered, "Nah, but I'll wrestle you for dessert."

Three of the hardest things in the world to say are:
1. I'm sorry
2. I was wrong
3. Where is the Worcestershire sauce?

A frantic man ran into a restaurant and yelled, "I'd like a crocodile sandwich, and make it snappy."

Kleptovers: The food that you secretly take home from a dinner or potluck with friends.

Why did the hipster burn his mouth? He drank the mochaccino frappa-latte-spresso before it was cool.

Mike McCrudgen: "Hey you, does this place serve crabs?"
Walter the Waiter: "Sure, we serve everyone."

What did the cupcake comedian say to the patrons at the café?
"You ain't seen Muffin yet."

If Lasagna made an action movie, what would it be called? Mission Impastable.

How do you keep a bagel from getting away? Put lox on it.

Why do mushrooms get invited to all the parties?
Because they are such fun guys.

What did the grape say when it got stepped on? Nothing, it just let out a little wine.

Carrots may be good for your eyes, but booze will double your vision.

What did Salvador Dali like to have for breakfast? Surreal.

Drunk: when you *feel* sophisticated but can't pronounce it.

Dejabrew: Recalling things you did while drunk.

"One time I was with my grandfather having breakfast at Denny's. The coffee was cold, the eggs were runny, hash browns were soggy, and the toast was burnt. As we were leaving, my grandfather said to the waitress, 'My compliments to the photographer.'" - Gary Mule Deer

"Grandma's cooking got so bad for a while that all the flies chipped in to get the screen door fixed." - Gary Mule Deer

Anything said before coffee cannot be used against me.

Funny Names

Tim Burr, Sue Flay, Robyn Banks, Paige Turner, Joe King,

Chaim Hungry, Krystal Ball, Hai Howa Yu, Amanda Lin,

Justin Case, Justin Tyme, Itsen Kreduhble, Eve N. Steven,

Eileen Dover, Ben Dover, Skip Dover, Haywood Yuhbuzof,

Albe Quick, Noah Lott, Rose Bush, Skip Town, Jack Tupp,

Iben Goofinov, Heezben Goofinov, Justin Idea, Nan Tuket,

Sharen Sharalike, Amanda Lovinkiss, Lois Price, Al Bino,

Jack Rabbit, Jack Cheese, Anita Bath, Harvey Walbanger,

Ella Vader, Art Nouveau, Anita Vacation, Noah Fence,

Dan Druff, Raya Light, Ann Chovie, Will Barol, Dor Bel,

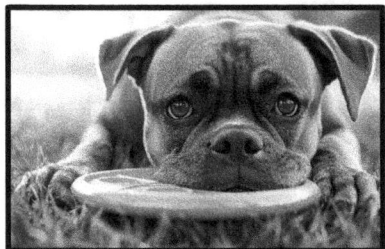

Ivana Frizbie, Ivana Peetzah,

Miss Behavin, Kenya Moovover,

Sue Perb, Betty Wont, Dela Ware,

Harry Fish, Patti Cake, Noah Scape, Don Key, Bill Fold,

Art Therupy, Paddy O'Furniture, Anita Plumber,

Alyson Wonderland, Frank Incense,

Ima Gonner, Ima Hogg, Bobbie Sox,

Tad Overdun,

Dayne Nite, Ali Katt, Claire Voyant,

Oliver Candy, Rose Garden, Will Power,

Helen Weelz, Laurel Lynn Hardi, Noah Pinion,

Hellen Bak, Izzy Gudinov, Camen Went, Penny Arkade,

Wendy Night, Rosy Cheeks, Pearl Harber, Lenda Hand,

Dee Zaster, Madam Idrathernot, Barb Dwier,

Mary Achie, Barry D. Hatchet, Rita Book,

Rhoda Harly, Luke Warm, Lisa May Hollar.

Funny Names of Towns in America

Dinosaur, Colorado

Whynot, North Carolina

Cut & Shoot, Texas - Uncertain, Texas - Ding Dong, Texas

Fries, Virginia - Hurt, Virginia

Concrete, Washington

Accident, Maryland

Climax, Michigan

Hell, Michigan

Cool, California - Rough and Ready, California

Okay, Oklahoma - Pink, Oklahoma - Hooker Oklahoma

Coward, South Carolina

Atomic City, Idaho

Last Chance, Iowa

Toad Suck, Arkansas

Rainbow City, Alabama

Santa Claus, Indiana

Normal, Illinois

Embarrass, Minnesota

Why, Arizona

Monkey's Eyebrow, Kentucky

Boring, Oregon

Chicken, Alaska

Good Ideas & Smart Questions

Why is "abbreviation" such a long word?

My friend said, "What rhymes with orange?" I said, "No it doesn't."

What word in the dictionary is always spelled incorrectly? Incorrectly.

Why do they put Braille dots on the keypad of the drive-up ATM?

Tradition is just peer pressure from dead people.

I looked up the word *opaque* in the dictionary.
It's not very clear.

Don't you hate it when people answer their own questions?
I certainly do.

What I if told you...
you read the top line wrong?

A man knocked on my door and asked for a small donation
for the local swimming pool. I gave him a glass of water.

Alice: "So, what's your opinion on Roe vs. Wade?"
Arlo: "Well, I prefer to float."

If you have an opinion about my life,
please raise your hand.
Now put it over your mouth.

I don't understand why all the ballerinas
dance on their toes. Why don't they just get taller women?

I only know 25 letters of the alphabet. I don't know Y.

Did you hear the joke about the roof?
Forget it, it's over your head.

I'm still trying to figure out why I was the only naked person at the gender reveal party.

I don't watch football, so I don't know who Taylor Swift is, but he sure sounds fast.

"You can trust pretty much everything you read on the internet." -Abraham Lincoln

Cigarettes are like squirrels. They're perfectly harmless until you put one in your mouth and light it on fire.

No matter how big and bad you are, when a three-year-old hands you a toy phone, you answer it.

The first rule in the passive aggressive club is…
You know what? Never mind. It's fine. Whatever.

Want some good advice?
Don't fry bacon naked.

Etcetera is a word used at the end of a sentence or idea to make it seem like you know a whole lot more than you do.

Whatever you do today, do it with the confidence of a 4-year-old in a Batman shirt.

Be careful when you follow the masses. The M might be silent.

Definition of a cell phone: A device used for looking less alone in public places.

Things that tell the truth: Seven-year-old boys, drunk people, and yoga pants.

"Analyzing humour is like dissecting a frog: Few people are interested and the frog dies." - EB white

What should you do if you're attacked by a gang of clowns? Go for the juggler.

Youniverse: A person who has no interest in anyone else and is endlessly fascinated by their own personal story.

You can't get mad at lazy people. They didn't do anything.

You may call it OCD, but I call it... "Put the damn tool back where you found it and shut the cabinet door!"

Healthy & Not So Healthy

Whenever I'm feeling blue, I just start breathing again.

Why did the cross-eyed teacher quit?
She couldn't control her pupils.

Why did the lady from the orange
juice factory lose her job?
She couldn't concentrate.

I went to the doctor with a suspicious-looking mole. He said
they all look like that, and I should just go home and leave
it in the garden.

What kind of exercise do lazy people do? Diddly-squats.

What did the dentist win at the dental competition?
A little plaque.

An apple a day keeps the
doctor away...
Or at least it does if you
throw it hard enough.

Dentist: "You need a crown."
Narcissistic patient: "Finally someone who gets me!"

Why don't blind people like skydiving?
It scares the hell out of their dogs.

My girlfriend left because she couldn't handle my OCD.
I told her to close the door five times on her way out.

"You've reached the Incontinence
Hotline. Hold, please."

I went to the foot doctor the other day.
He said, "Say ahhhhhhh."
I said, "Why?"
He said, "My dog just died."

I told my elderly mother, if she ever gets cold, just go stand in the corner where it's always 90 degrees.

Why did the man fall down the well? He couldn't see that well.

I got tired of being bald, so I bought a wig for $3 at the local thrift store. It was a small price toupee.

The best thing about being bald is that your bangs never get in your eyes, and it's easy to part your hair.

What do you call someone who can't stick with a diet? A desserter.

If life gives you melons, you might have dyslexia.

Who decided to make Dyslexia so hard to spell? The same person who thought it would be fun to add an "s" to the lisp.

Dyslexics of the world: Untie!

Having dyslexia can be problematic. One night I went to a toga party dressed as a goat.

A man goes into the doctor and says, "I think I have a hearing problem." The doctor asks, "Can you describe the symptoms?" The man replies, "Ok. Bart is a punk, Homer's a drunk, Marge has blue hair, Lisa's a..."

What does a zombie with dyslexia eat? Brians.

A man with a strawberry growing out of his head went to the doctor. The doctor carefully checked it out and said, "Let me give you some cream to put on that"

A nurse told the doctor, "There's a guy in the waiting room who is afraid he's become invisible. What should I tell him?" The doctor answered, "Tell him I can't see him today."

What do you give a man who has everything? Penicillin.

Did you hear about the man who lost his entire left side?
He's all right now.

My favorite Disney movie is "The Hunchback of Notre
Dame." I love a hero with a twisted back story.

"Mr. Smith, Dr. Woowoowitz
will see you now."
"Which doctor?"
"No, she's an M.D. like all the
others."

An old man shuffled into an ice
cream parlor, and with great effort and a lot of moaning,
pulled himself up onto a stool. After catching his breath, he
ordered a banana split. The waitress asked, "Crushed
nuts?"
"No, arthritis," he groaned."

What did one DNA molecule say to the other?
Do these genes make me look fat?

Home Life

My realtor sold me a two-story house: one story before the sale and a completely different story after!

I sold my vacuum. All it was doing was collecting dust.

When is a door not a door? When it's ajar.

What runs around a yard without moving? A fence.

Why was the plumber so tired? His work was draining.

Refrigenesia: When you find yourself standing in front of the open refrigerator, but you can't remember what you went there for.

I saw an advertisement that read: "Television for sale, $1, volume stuck on full." I thought to myself, "I can't turn that down!"

With great power comes great electricity bills.

My landlord says he needs to talk to me about the sky-high heating bills. I told him, "My door is always open."

Carl Contractor: "I can have that job done in three days." After one week, Hannah Homeowner spoke to him, "You said you could have this done in three days. What's up?" Carl Contractor: "I never said 3 consecutive days."

I went to buy camouflage sheets for my bed but couldn't find any.

I had the chance to buy real estate in Egypt, but it turned out to be a pyramid scheme.

"A perfect summer day is when the sun is shining, the breeze is blowing, the birds are singing, and the lawn mower is broken." - James Dent

Hotdogastan

Uncle Vojislav walked down the street with a pint of beer in each hand. He was inspired to sing a drinking song, but he couldn't get past the first two bars.

While driving along the coast of Hotdogastan, Uncle Vojislav saw a sign that said, "Watch for Rocks." *Now that's a pretty good deal*, he thought.

While driving through a small town, Uncle Vojislav saw a sign that said, "Watch for Children." *How barbaric!* he thought.

While driving through a forest to go bear hunting, Uncle Vojislav saw a sign, "BEAR LEFT," so he went home.

While walking through a village, Uncle Vojislav said to Uncle Drogoslav, "Look at that dog with one eye!" Uncle Vojislav covered one of his eyes and said, "Now what?"

How do you stop the Hotdogastan cavalry from charging? Unplug the carousel.

It was reported that a pickpocket stole the wallet of the Teeny Tiny Ambassador from Hotdogastan. It's hard to believe that someone could stoop that low.

Uncle Vojislav was in court. After 10 hours of trial he pleaded guilty. The judge said, "Why didn't you plead guilty at first and save us all this time? Uncle Vlatov said, "I thought I was innocent until I heard all the evidence."

Three Insults from Hotdogastan:

"You, sir, are a wart on the nose of humanity."

"You are the son of a motherless goat"

"Your face is so ugly it makes blind children cry."

Did you hear about the couple on a date in Hotdogastan? They froze to death outside a theater. They were waiting to see the movie "Heavy Snow. Closed for the Winter."

Why do people from Hotdogastan hate making chocolate chip cookies? It takes too long to peel the M&Ms.

A young woman said to her mother, "Is it true that in Hotdogastan, the bride doesn't even know the husband until they get married?" The mother sighed, "Alas, that's true everywhere."

A professor and a custodian were lounging next to each other on a Hotdogastan beach. The professor leaned over and said, "Hello Neighbor. Have you read Marx?" The custodian sighed, "Yes. They're from these lounge chairs!"

The Teeny Tiny Ambassador from Hotdogastan made his way to the Sunny Side Nudist Colony in Palm Springs, but he was asked to leave after a few days because he kept sticking his nose in everybody's business.

It is said that the Tiny Ambassador from Hotdogastan has an uncontrollable habit of farting in every elevator he steps into. That's wrong on so many levels.

Where does General Zitami of Hotdogastan keep his armies? Up his sleevies.

General Zitami

A man from Hotdogastan saw a letter on his doormat with the words, "DO NOT BEND" on the envelope. He spent the next 2 hours trying to figure out how to pick it up.

What do they call a baby's wave in Hotdogastan? A Microwave.

Immature Butt Fun

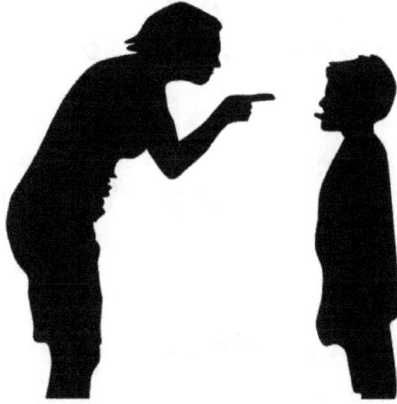

What do you call someone who refuses to fart in public?
A private tutor.

Why did the toilet paper roll down the hill?
To get to the bottom!

What do you call a person with only a head? A Nobody.

What's brown and sounds like a bell? Dung!

Which one is faster, hot or cold? Hot. You can catch a cold.

How do you stop a baby astronaut from crying?
You rocket.

What's a vampire's favorite fruit? A neck-tarine!

Is buttcheeks one word or should I spread them apart?

What do you call a drunk dinosaur? A staggersaurus.

A plane crashed in the jungle and every single person died.
Who survived? Married couples.

What do you call a blind deer? No eye deer.

Why does a duck have feathers?
To cover up his buttquack.

I always knock on the fridge door before opening it, just in
case there's a salad dressing.

What's the difference between roast beef and pea soup?
Anyone can roast beef, but very few people can pee soup.

What city has the worst body odor? Pittsburgh.

What did the ghost put on his bagel? Scream cheese.

My girlfriend told me I was immature and needed to grow up. Guess who's not allowed in my treehouse anymore!

Why did the security officer smell so bad?
He was on duty.

What did the Llama say to her boyfriend as they prepared for a picnic? Alpaca lunch.

Music

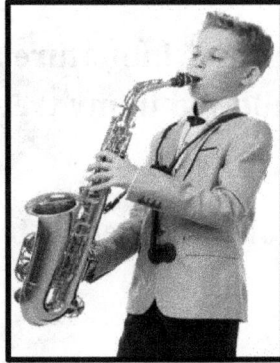

I don't allow my kids to watch the orchestra.
Too much sax and violins.

What musical instrument is kept in your bathroom?
A tuba toothpaste.

What do you get when you drop a piano down a mineshaft?
A-flat minor.
How about a mine shaft at a military base?
A-flat major.

Why couldn't Mozart find his best friend? He was Haydn.

Man knocks on door.
Man: Hello Ma'am, I'm the piano tuner.
Woman: I didn't send for a piano tuner.
Man: No, but your neighbors did.

Why do bagpipe players walk while they play? They're trying to escape the noise.

What's full of keys but can't open a door? A piano.

How is a banjo solo like an artillery shell? By the time you hear it coming, it's too late to run.

What's the difference between a banjo and an onion?
No one cries when you chop up a banjo.

Two windmills on a hill: One says to the other, "I enjoy classical music. How 'bout you?" The other replies, "I'm a big metal fan."

Steal a man's wallet and he'll be poor for a day. Teach him to play guitar and he'll be poor for a lifetime.

What do you call it when a musical spider regrows a limb quickly? Allegro.

My next-door neighbors listen to loud, wild music... whether they like it or not.

Dad: "Son, it's time to do your homework and turn off that Korean dance music, whatever you call it."   Son: "K Pop."

I was in a band called *Teenager's Bed*. We never made it.

The difference between a drummer and a mutual fund? The mutual fund will mature & make money, eventually.

What's the difference between jazz and rock guitarists? Rock guitarists play 3 chords in front of thousands of people. Jazz guitarists play thousands of chords in front of 3 people.

Girl: Dad, what music did you like growing up?
Dad: I was a big Zeppelin fan.
Girl: The Band?
Dad: Them too.
Girl: Who?
Dad: Not so much.

Ok Boomer!

What do you call a Boomer at a rap concert? Lost.

Man: What does your husband do for a living?
Lady: My husband's dead.
Man: What did he do before he died?
Lady: He clutched at his chest, moaned, and fell over.

What goes up but never comes down? Your age.

Why did the boomer cross the road?
She forgot where she parked the car.

As you grow older, do you miss the innocence and idealism of your youth, or do you mostly miss the cherry bombs?

What did the bald Boomer say when he was given a comb for his birthday? "Gee, thanks. I'll never part with this."

I saw my doctor last week. He referred me to a paleontologist.

I hate seeing old people... then realizing I went to high school with them.

An elderly couple were at a party. The wife leaned over and whispered to her husband, "I just let out a long, silent fart. What should I do?" The husband replied, "First off, replace the batteries in your hearing aid!"

"Uncle Wilber died of asbestos poisoning. It took a long time to cremate him." - Tommy Cooper

Wife: I was a fool when I married you!
Husband: Yes, you were! But, I was too young and in love at the time to care.

Have you heard the new country song for seniors? It's called *I've fallen for you, baby, but I can't get up.*

Yoda: "Do or do not; there is no try."
Baby Yoda: "OK boomer."

I still remember the last words my grandfather ever said to me: "Don't mess with the ladder, you idiot!"

I asked my grandma which walker she preferred. She said, "Johnny."

An 85-year-old man with bad hearing went to the doctor.
Doctor: It appears you have a heart murmer.
The man went home to his wife.
Wife: How was the doctor visit?
Man: Strange. Have the two of you met?
Wife: No, why?
Man: He told me I have a hot mama.

"How young can you die of old age?" - Steven Wright

The older I get, the earlier it gets late.

They're not gray hairs.
They're wisdom highlights.

What's a Boomer's favorite
underwear? Depends.

Now that I've gotten older, everything has begun to click.
My knees, my neck, my ankles...

I saw an ear doctor today, but I think I'll get a second
opinion. Why on earth would I need a heron egg?

What do you call a snowman
when he gets old? A puddle.

Why do boomers make horrible
cashiers? They're afraid of
change.

A 95-year-old old man sat next to an old lady at a bar. He smiled at her and said, "So, do I come here often?"

What do you call someone who enjoys Mondays? Retired.

A 104-year-old woman was being interviewed on TV. She was asked what was the best thing about being 104? After some thought, she answered, "No peer pressure."

Philosophy

"A conclusion is the place where you got tired of thinking."
- Steven Wright

My father always used to say, "In life, when one door closes, another one will open." He was a great philosopher, but an awful cabinet maker.

Don't sweat the petty things and don't pet the sweaty things.

Some days you're the dog. Some days you're the hydrant.

What is the most common question that a person holding a PhD in Philosophy asks other people?
"Would you like fries with that?"

What's the difference between ignorance and apathy?
Don't know. Don't care.

The trouble with the rat race is that even if you win, you're still a rat.

The early bird gets the worm, but it's the second mouse who gets the cheese.

Worrying works! Here's my proof: 99% of the things I worry about never happen.

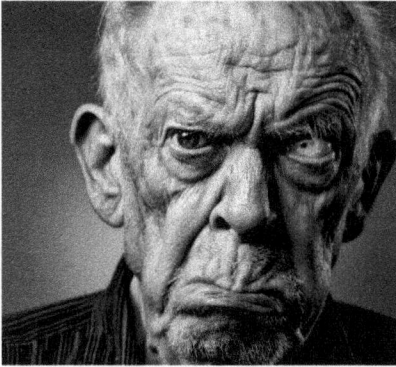

Time may be a great healer, but it's a lousy beautician.

Was it hard to adopt nihilism as your personal philosophy?
Nah, there was nothing to it.

"Never try to teach a pig to sing. It wastes your time and annoys the pig."
– Italian Proverb

Time is what keeps everything from happening at once.

Change is inevitable, except from a vending machine.

A good time to keep your mouth shut is when you're in deep water.

PIRATES

What did the pirate say on his 80th birthday? Aye Matey!

Why couldn't the sweet little children watch the pirate movie? Because it was rated AARRRRR!
Why was it rated R?
Too much booty.

Isn't it ironic that the *Pirates of the Caribbean* movie has a piracy warning?

Why was the pirate ship so cheap?
It was on sail.

Where do pirate captains get their hooks?
Secondhand shops.

Why does it take pirates so long
to learn the alphabet? Because
they can spend years at C.

Did you hear about the red pirate ship that collided with
the blue pirate ship? All the pirates were marooned.

What do you call a pirate who likes to skip school?
Captain Hooky!

Why did the pirate go to the Apple store?
He needed a new iPatch.

How do you make a pirate mad?
Take away the "p."

Relationships

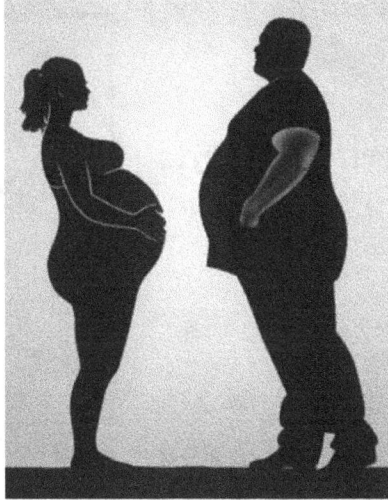

I told my wife she should embrace her mistakes, so she gave me a big hug.

Why didn't the newlyweds go to the gym?
Because some relationships don't work out.

Two telephone line workers got married.
The wedding was just OK, but the reception was amazing!

A woman phoned her neighbor and said: "You ought to close your curtains the next time you and your wife are snuggling. The whole street was watching and laughing at you yesterday." To which the man replied: "Well the joke's on all you because I wasn't even at home yesterday!"

My girlfriend isn't talking to me. She said I ruined her birthday. I'm not sure how. I didn't even remember it was her birthday.

My wife says I'm getting fatter, but in my defense, I've had a lot on my plate lately.

I've got a buddy who weighs 275 pounds, and dates both men and women. He's bi and large, a good person.

I like to hold hands at the movies… which always seems to startle strangers.

My wife and I laugh about how competitive we are. But I laugh more... and louder.

Women are nicer than men. If a woman says, "smell this," it usually smells nice.

Ron: "How can a farmer like me get a girl like Mary Sue?"
John: "A Tractor."

My boyfriend started a bee farm to help save the bees. I think he's a keeper.

Definition of "No offense but…": What I'm about to say is definitely going to offend you.

I have to be very careful. My ex told me, "The last thing I want to do is hurt you... but it's still on the list."

My girlfriend said she's leaving me because I keep pretending to be a Transformer. I said, "No, wait! I can change!"

Relationships are like algebra, you examine your X and try to figure out Y.

The difference between love and marriage: Love is blind. Marriage is an eye-opener.

"A study in the New York Times says that women have better verbal skills than men. I just want to say to the authors of that survey... duh." - Conan O'Brien

Definition of Askhole: Someone who constantly asks for your advice, yet always does the opposite.

I made my wife's dreams come true when we got married in a castle. But you wouldn't have known it from the look on her face as we were bouncing around.

I told my wife she was drawing her eyebrows too high. She looked surprised.

"That's Nice": What you say when you realize you've zoned out in the middle of another person's story.

They say marriages are made in heaven. But so are thunder and lightning. - Clint Eastwood

A Scottish man went to a Halloween party wearing a girl on his back. He threw open the door and announced, "I'm a turtle!" A man sneered, "How can you be a turtle? You've got is a girl on your back?" "That's not just any girl," the Scotsman grinned, "That's Michelle!"

A 60-year-old man and woman were celebrating their wedding anniversary at the beach when the woman found an ornate bottle in the sand. She picked it up, popped the cork, and out came a blue genie, who said to them, "You have freed me from a thousand years of captivity. In return, I shall give you both any wish you desire." The woman said, "I've always wanted to travel the world!" The genie snapped his fingers, and in her hand appeared a round-the-world airline ticket. Then the man whispered in the genie's ear, "I've always wanted a wife that was 30 years younger than me." The genie snapped his fingers, and instantly the man was 90.

Mantrum: A man acting like a child and throwing a tantrum, usually for some mundane and stupid reason.

Sally Smith said to her husband, Lester, "Look at our neighbors Billy and Brenda Brown. They're so loving. See how they're always hugging, and see how he kisses her when he gets home from work. Why don't you do that?" Lester thought a moment and replied, "Well, I guess I could, but I hardly know her."

God said to Abraham, come forth and I shall give you a wife. But Abraham came in 5th and only got a toaster. (And Abraham rejoiced.)

Religion

So what if I don't know what Armageddon means?
It's not the end of the world.

A Buddhist monk asked, "Master, is it okay for a monk to use emails?" "Yes, son," the guru smiled, "as long as there are no attachments."

"Jesus loves you," is a nice thing to hear in church, not so much in an El Salvadorian prison.

Buddhist Master: "I've never met anyone as thoughtless as you in my entire life."
Disciple: "Thank you, Master!"

"God, how long is a million years?"
"To me, it is but one second."
"God, how much is a million dollars?"
"To me, it is but a penny."
"God, may I have a penny?"
"Wait a minute..."

"Dear Lord, lead me not unto temptation—I can find that myself."

What do you call a Vatican priest who sleepwalks? A roamin' Catholic.

Why did the Buddhist monk go to Las Vegas? Because he loves Tibet.

What do martial arts and Passover matzah have in common? Ju-dough.

How does a rabbi make his coffee? Hebrews it.

What cheese is served at the Passover Seder? Matzah-rella.

At church on Sunday, the minister raised his hands in the air and ended his sermon by preaching, "...and so I say unto you, that compared to the Almighty, we humans are but dust..."

A moment later, little Sally turned to her mother and whispered, "Mom, what's butt dust?"

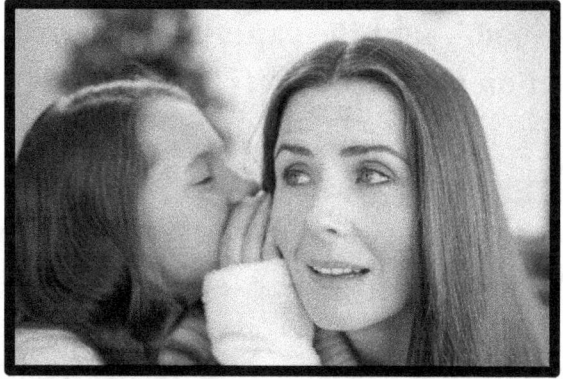

My favorite prayer:
"Lord, help us to be the people our dogs think we are."

A Jewish woman stood up mid-flight from New York to L.A. and shouted, "Is there a doctor on board?"
A nice-looking young man rushed over and said: "I am a doctor. How can I help?"
She replied: "I'd like you to meet my daughter?"

A nun had the hiccups for an entire week. Finally, she went to see the doctor. He did some tests and told her she was pregnant. Turns out she wasn't, but it sure cured her hiccups.

As a storm raged at sea, the captain realized his ship was sinking, so he shouted, "Anyone here know how to pray?" One guy stepped forward and said, "Aye, captain, I know how to pray."

"Good," said the captain. "You pray while the rest of us put on our life jackets – we're one jacket short."

If atheism was a business, what kind would it be?
A Non-prophet.

What kind of car would Jesus drive? A Christ-ler.

Moses was the first person to use control-C as a shortcut.

Where does it mention baseball in the bible?
Chapter 1, Verse 1. In the big inning...

I don't know if Facebook has ever caused the lame to walk, but it's sure caused the dumb to speak.

Buddhist Monk: Buddha, tell us what makes us human.
Buddha: Select all images with traffic lights.

Did you hear about the dyslexic cow in India that became enlightened? It repeated Oooommm for 20 years.

Is a rivalry between two Hindus still considered beef?

After taking a class in the history of Hinduism, all I have to say is, "Holy cow!"

Most people know about Samson, the strong biblical warrior. But he had a dad, Samsonite, who was an even tougher case.

I definitely want Brooklyn [his son] to be Christened, but I don't know into what religion yet. - David Beckham

One day God and Devil were walking down the road. God said, "I have an idea how to get people to worship me. I think I'll call it religion." The Devil cheered and replied, "Wonderful. I'll organize it for you!"

Jeff and Liza went to Swami Salami's Spiritual Retreat Center in Maui. On the third night, Jeff found Liza in the lodge, under the blanket, snuggling with the great Swami himself. All three of them were shocked, but the Swami quickly put a finger in the air and said with great wisdom, "Wait! Before you jump to conclusions, who are you going to trust, me or your own eyes?"

When does life actually begin? According to the Jewish tradition, the embryo is not considered viable until it graduates from medical school.

What do you call a schizophrenic Buddhist? A person who is at two with the universe.

What state has the most Muslims? Allahbama.

What do Jewish dogs do when they reach 13 years old? They have a Bark Mitzvah.

Two cannibals met one day on a jungle path. The first one said, "I went up the river and trapped two Catholic priests. I brought them home and boiled them, but they tasted terrible." His friend said, "Wait, you boiled them?"
"Yeah, why?"
"Didn't you know, those were friars?"

The associate minister unveiled the church's new campaign slogan last Sunday: "I upped my pledge – Up Yours!"

Church Newsletter: Bertha Belch, a missionary from Africa, will be speaking tonight at Calvary Methodist. Come hear Bertha Belch all the way from Africa.

"If only God would give me some clear sign! Like making a large deposit in my name at a Swiss Bank." - Woody Allen

What goes CLOP CLOP CLOP, BANG BANG, CLOP CLOP CLOP? An Amish drive-by shooting.

Heck: The place you go if you don't believe in Gosh.

On his death bed, an old Jewish man said to his wife, "Oh, Sarah, when the shop burned down, you were right beside me."

"Yes, I was, Moshe," she replied.

"When the Nazis drove us out of our home in Germany, you were beside me again."

"That's true, Moshe."

"And now you're at my death bed."

"I am, darling."

"Well, I'm starting to think you're bad luck, Sarah."

What is black and white, black and white, black and white?
A nun rolling down a hill.

A burglar was tiptoeing through a house one night when he heard someone say, "Jesus is watching you." He took a few more steps and heard it again, "Jesus is watching you."

Then he noticed a caged parrot in the corner.

He stepped to the bird, looked him over and said, "What's your name bird?"

The parrot answered, "Moses."

The burglar chuckled, "What kind of family would name its parrot Moses?"

The bird answered, "The kind of family that would name its Rottweiler Jesus."

Science

Who is this Rorschach dude and why is he so good at making pictures of my mom tormenting me?

Neil DeGrasse Tyson, Stephen Hawking, and Bill Nye walk into a church. Neil and Bill look at Stephen and yell, "My God, Stephen, you're cured!"

A photon was going through airport security. The TSA agent asked if he had any luggage.
The photon said, "No, I'm traveling light."

How much does a rainbow weigh?
Not much. It's pretty light.

Light travels faster than sound, which is why some people seem bright until you hear them talk.

Don't trust atoms, they make up everything.

Does the name Pavlov ring a bell?

Why is a moon rock tastier than an earth rock?
Because it's a little meteor.

Albert Einstein developed a theory about space. And it was about time too.

Why are astronauts so clean?
They take meteor showers.

I love the way the earth rotates.
It really makes my day.

How does an astronaut keep his pants up?
Asteroid belts.

What did one tectonic plate say when it bumped into the other tectonic plate? "Sorry, my fault."

For scientists, what's the most horrifying word in nuclear physics? Oops!

One cold winter morning, a woman in Montana texted her husband who was working in L.A. She wrote: "Windows frozen, won't open."
Husband texts back: "You need to slowly pour some lukewarm water over it."
Wife texts back five minutes later: "Uh... oh no! The computer's really messed up now."

Screwing in a Light Bulb

How many gorillas does it take to screw in a light bulb?
Only one, but it takes a lot of light bulbs!

How many mystery writers does it take to screw in a light
bulb? Two. One to screw it almost all the way in
and the other to give it a surprise twist at the end.

How many grad students does it take to change a bulb?
Only one, but it will probably take ten years.

How many telemarketers does it take to change a bulb?
Only one, but he has to do it while you're eating dinner.

How many country singers do you need to change a light bulb? Two. One to change it and the other to sing about the good ol' days with the old bulb.

How many real estate agents does it take to change a light bulb? Ten, but we'll accept eight.

How many skateboarders does it take to change a bulb? One, but it takes him 213 tries.

How many alcoholics does it take to change a light bulb? Two. One holds the bulb and the other drinks until the room spins.

How many punk rockers does it take to change a light bulb? Two. One to change it and the other to eat the old bulb.

How many narcissists does it take to change a light bulb? One. He holds the bulb while the world revolves around him.

How many agnostics does it take to change a light bulb? We can't know for sure.

How many psychologists does it take to change a bulb? Only one, but the light bulb has to really *want* to change.

How many flies does it take to screw in a light bulb? Two, but nobody knows how they got in there.

How many mechanics does it take to change a light bulb? Three. One to check the bulb, one to acquire the wrong part, and one to tell you that it won't be done until Tuesday.

How many babysitters does it take to change a light bulb? None. Pampers don't come that small.

How many folks from Hotdogastan does it take to screw in a light bulb? Four. One to hold the bulb and three to turn the chair.

How many surgeons does it take to change a light bulb? One, but first he'll remove the socket, then pull out the wiring, and in the end, he'll give you a flashlight to use for the rest of your life.

Sports

It was dinnertime and my wife asked me if I had seen the dog bowl. I answered, "I didn't even know he could."

What lights up a soccer stadium? A match.

I heard a funny joke about a boomerang, but I forgot it. Oh well, it will come back to me.

Arguing with strangers online is like wrestling sharks. Even if you win, it was a really stupid thing to do.

Why was Cinderella so lousy at baseball? Because she ran away from the ball, and she had a pumpkin for a coach.

Two silkworms are in a wrestling match. It ended in a tie.

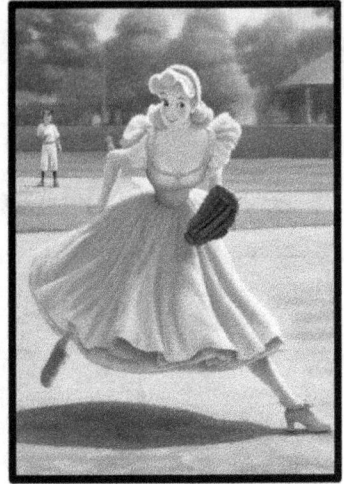

What's brown and bad for your teeth? A baseball bat.

Cross country skiing is easier if you live in a small country. - Steven Wright

What is the hardest thing about skateboarding? The concrete.

Give a man a fish and he'll eat for a day. Teach a man to fish and he'll sit in a little boat and drink beer all day.

My computer beat me at chess, but it was no match for me at kickboxing. - Emo Phillips

I went to a fight and a hockey game broke out.

Why do hipsters love field hockey? Because it's ice hockey before it gets cool.

If at first you don't succeed, maybe you should skip skydiving.

Soccer is a strange game. It's a bunch of people running away from their own goals.

What did the football player say to the flight attendant? "Put me in coach."

Every morning I announce that I'm going running but then I don't go. It's a running joke.

Who was the skateboarders' favorite boxer? Muhammad Ollie.

What's the difference between time and a ball hog? Time passes.

Time to Make Like A...

Time to make like a cloud and let it all drift away.

Time to make like a sponge and soak it all in.

Time to make like a door and shut it all behind you.

Time to make like a key and unlock new opportunities.

Time to make like a tree and leave.

Time to make like a bad check and bounce.

Time to make like a shepherd and get the flock out of here.

Time to make like a Winnebago and motor home.

Time to make like a bakery truck and haul buns.

Time to make like a chef and get the fork out of here.

Time to make like a deck of cards and shuffle away.

Time to make like a hippie and blow this joint.

Time to make like a banana and split.

Time to make like a scale and go weigh.

Time to make like a fridge and chill out.

Time to make like a bladder and piss off.

Time to make like Tom and cruise.

Time to make like Santa Claus and leave your presence.

Time to make like a fetus and head out.

Time to make like my dad and disappear.

Time to make like a nylon and run.

Time to make like a tootsie and roll.

Time to make like a goalie and get the puck out of here.

Time to make like a fart and slip out.

Time to make like a toad and go croak.

Time to make like a horse turd and hit the trail.

Time to make like an astronaut and blast off.

Time to make like a dog with worms and scoot.

Time to make like a coyote and scat.

Time to make like traffic and jam.

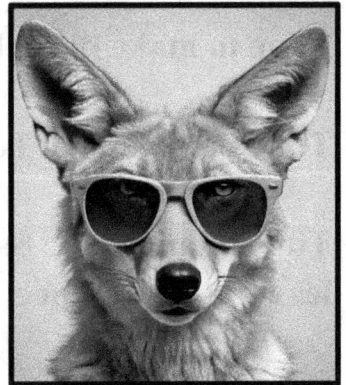

Time to make like a drum and beat it.

Time to make like a library and book.

Time to make like a rock n roll.

Time to make like yo mama's pants and split!

Work

A magician was walking down the street, and he turned into a grocery store.

What do you call a line of men waiting to get haircuts? A barberqueue.

I've heard that 90% of lawyers give the rest a bad name.

Why can't accountants get library cards? Because they're book-keepers.

What do you call a pudgy psychic? A four-chin teller.

I lost my job. Now I am so poor I can't even pay attention.

What's the difference between jelly and jam? You can't jelly 12 clowns into a tiny car.

Why are lawyers buried 6' deep? Because deep down, they're really good people.

Politicians and diapers should both be changed regularly— and for the same reason.

I used to be a banker, but I lost interest.

I used to be a baker, but I couldn't make enough dough.

Wood fired pizza. Now Pizza is desperately looking for work.

Did you hear about the farmer who drove his tractor while drunk? It was really whisky.

My boss told me to have a good day, so I went home.

I didn't want to believe that my dad was stealing from his job at the transportation department, but when I got home all the signs were there.

I tried to make a living as a barber, but I couldn't cut it.

A lawsuit and a banjo have something in common. Everyone is happy when the case is closed.

I like what road workers wear... overall.

What did the janitor say when he jumped out of the closet? "Supplies!"

Did you hear the one about the blind carpenter? He was cured when he picked up his hammer and saw.

They all laughed when I said I wanted to become a professional comedian. Well, they're not laughing now!
- Bob Monkhouse

Uncle John walked into a lumberyard and asked for some two-by-fours. The clerk asked, "How long do you need them?" Uncle John answered, "About 40 years. We're building a house."

My boss yelled at me. He said I'd never amount to much because I procrastinate so much. I said, "Just you wait!"

What was the name of the carpenter who built King Arthur's round table? Sir Cumference.

Why did the candle quit her job?
She was feeling burned out.

I couldn't work today because of an eye problem. I just can't see myself working today.

To the person who stole my copy of Microsoft Office, I will find you. You have my Word.

"I am Buzz Aldrin, NASA astronaut and second man to step on the moon. Neil before me."

The CEO of Ikea was appointed Prime Minister of Sweden. He's currently assembling his cabinet.

I just found out the company that produces yardsticks won't be making them any longer.

Morrie the plumber fixed a leaking faucet at the surgeon's house. It was $150 for a two-minute job. The surgeon exclaimed, "I don't even charge that amount, and I am a brain surgeon!" The plumber smirked, "I didn't either when I was a surgeon. That's why I switched to plumbing."

What is a plumber's least favorite vegetable? Leeks.

I asked a tech guy, "How do you make a Motherboard?"
He said, "I tell her about my job."

My boss told me that there's no such thing as problems, only opportunities. I said: "Well, I have a serious drinking opportunity."

Sometimes I think back on all the people I've lost along the way and remember why I stopped being a tour guide in Death Valley.

My grandfather was a veterinarian and a taxidermist. He had a little sign at the desk that said, "No matter what, you'll get your dog back."

Did you hear about the optometrist who fell into his lens grinder? He made a spectacle of himself.

Zimply Brilliant Quotations

A clear conscience is usually the sign of a bad memory.
 - Steven Wright

I am not afraid of death, I just don't want to be there when
it happens. - Woody Allen

Never underestimate the power of stupid people in large
groups. - George Carlin

When you enter his room, you have to kiss his ring. I don't
mind, but he has it in his back pocket. - Don Rickles

Why do they call it rush hour when no one moves?
- Robin Williams

I'm not for everyone. I'm barely for me. - Marc Maron

The Swiss have an interesting army. Five hundred years without a war. Pretty impressive. Also pretty lucky for them. Ever seen that little Swiss Army knife they have to fight with? Not much of a weapon there. Corkscrews. Bottle openers. "Come on, buddy, let's go. You get past me, the guy in the back of me, he's got a spoon. Back off, I've got the toe clippers right here too." - Jerry Seinfeld

Before you criticize a man, walk a mile in his shoes. That way, when you do criticize him, you'll be a mile away and have his shoes.
- Steve Martin

Everything is changing. People are taking their comedians seriously and the politicians as a joke. - Will Rogers

A guy complains of a headache. Another guy says, "Do what I do. I put my head on my wife's bosom, and the headache goes away." The next day, the man says, "Did you do what I told you to?" "Yep, I sure did. By the way, you have a nice house!" - Henny Youngman

I think it's the duty of the comedian to find out where the line is drawn and cross it deliberately. - George Carlin

I'm happier than a tornado in a trailer park.
- Larry the Cable Guy

I haven't spoken to my wife in years. I just didn't want to interrupt her.
- Rodney Dangerfield

Behind every great man is a woman rolling her eyes.
- Jim Carrey

Maybe there is no actual place called hell. Maybe hell is just having to listen to your grandparents breathe through their noses when they're eating sandwiches. - Jim Carrey

Looking at cleavage is like looking at the sun. You don't stare at it. It's too risky. You get a sense of it and then you look away. - Jerry Seinfeld

My grandmother is over ninety and still doesn't need glasses. Drinks right out of the bottle. - Henny Youngman

The End

A note from the Author

Great jokes are like precious gems. We want to keep them, and treasure them. When we bring them out at the right time, in the midst of a conversation, they fill the room with intelligence, wit, and mainly, fun.

The following pages are for jokes that you've found, overheard, made up... Keep them here, in this little book, so you will be able to remember and appreciate them your entire life!

www.ingramcontent.com/pod-product-compliance
Lightning Source LLC
Chambersburg PA
CBHW050528280326
41933CB00011B/1508